Consider This...

By: Marcus Brewster

Consider This...

Published*Edited*Interior Design by:
Shawn K Publishing
Shawnkpublishing@gmail.com

ISBN for Print Version: 978-1-7353066-5-0

Printed in the United States of America

Your positive book reviews are appreciated!

Acknowledgements

I would like to thank My Mother, also known as My Favorite Girl, LaVerne Brewster, for being my number one fan. You would not be reading this book today, if it wasn't for her.

To Wesley and Nicolas Brewster. My sons, and my reasons for existing. Know that everything your daddy does, is for the betterment of you two. This book would not be here today without you.

To Shawn Karawa, at Shawn K Publishing. Thank you for walking with me on the road to becoming an author. This is just the beginning.

Finally, I would like to thank my unofficial mentors, Percy Miller aka Master P and Dame Dash, as well as Michael Eric Dyson, Cathy Hughes, and the Late Great Nipsey Hussle. All of these individuals have provided me with so much inspiration, and knowledge; that have given me the confidence to "Consider This..." thing called entrepreneurship. It could not be done without you guys paving the way.

Table of Contents

Intro

In every major city throughout the United States, there are different sections of the city that represent an entire people, with a display of that group's prosperity. Think about this- almost every major city has a "Chinatown." You have "Spanish Harlem" in New York City. You have "Little Italy" in cities like New York City, Baltimore MD, and San Diego CA.

Now answer this question: *What is the "Black Area" in every major city?* They are normally impoverished areas, with low value, and high crime rates; and they normally do not have any black-owned businesses in the neighborhood.

Now think about this- plenty of businesses and consumers keep their dollars circulating in their cultural communities. The average lifespan of a dollar in the Asian community is 28 days; in the Jewish community it is 19 days; and in the African American community it is six hours. Why is this? For as long as I can remember, it has never been a priority in the black community to go against the status quo. That is, you graduate high school- you go to college- then you get a job. Either that or you graduate high school, then go right in the workforce.

Years ago, I knew a Caucasian young man who was in medical school at the time, who told me his mom used to show him how to cut meat while at the dinner table. He said his mom would have him cut his meat with precision, as he was being groomed to be a surgeon. It is this type of training, and encouragement, that I believe we lack in the black community. We don't really instill in our children that greatness is available to them, outside of sports and entertainment. However, that ends today. If you are reading this, then you, your parents, a mentor, etc. believe there is a different way you can achieve greatness; and today is the first day of the rest of your life.

Who or What is an Entrepreneur?

Let me tell you two stories about two people I went to high school with. One of them was a young lady I called "Candy Girl." The other was a young man, named "Kelbo."

Candy Girl was a young lady in high school that used to sell "Airheads." She would buy a big box from Costco, or one of the other wholesalers, and sell the individual contents for twenty-five cents. So, if the box of Airheads was five dollars, with fifty individual Airheads in it, at twenty-five cent per, that is twelve dollars and fifty cents, which ended up being a seven dollar profit.

Kelbo was a young man who started his own clothing line back in 1998-99, before it was the thing to do. The name of his company was "Hot Pursuit." What Kelbo would do was design things like hoodies, t-shirts, sweatpants, etc. with glue, paint, and glitter products. The beautiful thing about his set up was the customer would provide the clothing to him, he would design it, and they would pay him for it.

It was actually genius, because he did not have the responsibility of the "cost of goods" expenses. (Cost of goods refers to the money it costs to purchase the clothing.) All he had to do was pay for the glue, glitter, and paint, which in the grand scheme of things, is considerably less than what he would have made if he also had to purchase the clothes.

Almost every piece of clothing he made and candy she sold, depending on what they charged, was ALWAYS going to produce a profit. Regardless of if they were selling candy, clothes, or providing a service. While I did not recognize, or even knew what it was at that time, I later would learn that Candy Girl and Kelbo, at the ages of fourteen and sixteen, were entrepreneurs.

Now that we have a couple of examples, let me explain to you exactly what is an entrepreneur? The dictionary defines an entrepreneur as "an individual who creates a new business, bearing most of the risk and enjoying most of the rewards... Entrepreneurship that proves to be successful in taking on the risk of creating a startup is rewarded with profits, fame, and continued growth opportunities."

How does Candy Girl and Kelbo compare to the definition of an entrepreneur? Start with "an individual who creates a business."

In high school, when I was coming up (1996-2000), there were no vending machines in the school, thus increasing the demand for snacks, which she supplied.

Next, "bearing most of the risk." Kelbo had the risk of messing up someone's clothing. While he did not supply the clothing, if he did a bad job, he risked losing not only the money for the decorating supplies, but the money he may have to compensate the customer if he messed up their clothing. Candy Girl also had risks. The risk was purchasing the product without assurance that they would sell. Not to mention, could potentially have her product taken away by school officials.

Finally, "enjoying most of the reward." In this instance, she enjoyed all the reward because once the product is paid for, all the profit is hers. She had no partners to split revenue with. There also were not a lot of expenses as far as production costs etc. Strictly the cost of goods, which always sold out. The same thing went for Kelbo. His biggest expense was paint/glitter/glue, which at the time, was not a lot of cost, and because he had minimum cost, he received a large profit, from a percentage standpoint.

The one thing the definition of entrepreneur does not state is an age limit, on when you can be one. Candy Girl knew at fourteen years old, that she did not need a job to earn money. Kelbo learned at sixteen, the same valuable lesson. Which I am sure he has benefited them, to this day.

The Ugly History of Black Prosperity

Do you know how wealthy we have been as a people? No? Now is the perfect time for a little history lesson. For starters, let's take it all the way back to Africa. Back to a time when our people were kings and queens. Our very existence before, the country was invaded, and our ancestors placed in captivity, was that of royalty. Hard to think that it could get worse than that, right. While surpassing slavery on the horrific scale is a tall task, that does not mean an attempt has not been made. Let's fast forward a couple of hundred years to 1921, to one of America's worst moments, and discuss "Black Wall Street."

In Tulsa, Oklahoma there was an area known as the Greenwood District, that was one of the richest African American communities in the United States, famously known as Black Wall Street. The Greenwood District was over forty acres of land. Just to give you an example of how financially powerful African Americans were during that time. In 1921, the entire state of Oklahoma had two airports. However, six African American families in the Greenwood District owned their own planes.

The airline industry has always been one of the most lucrative industries. Today that industry is worth 1.7 trillion dollars, so imagine how much money an African American family had to have, in order to be a part of that industry, let alone six of them. Ladies and Gentlemen, that was Black Wall Street.

Unfortunately, all good things ALWAYS come to an end, and Black Wall Street was no exception, because on May 31, 1921, the worst incident of racial violence in American history, occurred with the Tulsa Race Riots/Massacre.

It started over the accusation of assault from a seventeen-year-old white girl, against a nineteen-year-old black man. If this story sounds familiar, it should. History is filled with black men's lives ending because of allegations of sexual misconduct by white women.

However, that is another story for another day-- back to the Tulsa Massacre. While rumors of the alleged assault swirling, an angry white mob formed outside of the courthouse where the alleged defendant was being held. Subsequently, angry, black citizens also began to congregate outside of the courthouse. Fights between the two groups ensued. Shots were fired, and a dozen people were killed.

News spread about the deaths outside of the courthouse, and before martial law was declared, the white population began mobbing through Black Wall Street, rioting, killing, burning, and looting homes and businesses throughout the night. The next morning, black prosperity as we knew it in Tulsa, Oklahoma, was no more. Destroyed were thirty-five square blocks of buildings (homes and businesses) of black grocery store owners, doctors, maintenance workers, bankers, and entrepreneurs. Leaving thousands of black people homeless.

As much as people love to talk about Black Wall Street, one event that doesn't get a lot of press is the "Wilmington Coup of 1898." While this incident was not economic base, the outcome of the damage was the same as Black Wall Street. This time, the act of domestic terrorism, was based on the power structure.

At the time, 90+ percent of Wilmington's political figures were black, or biracial. Again, a white mob overthrew black political leaders from the city, destroyed the property and businesses of black citizens, while killing up to three hundred people. This seemingly is the only incident of its kind in American history, as no other incident resulted in the immediate removal and replacement of elected officials.

These are just a couple of examples of the majority not wanting to see us prosper. And though these examples are a little dated, you don't have to go far to see how ugly things STILL for black people are, particularly from a financial standpoint. We are still being deprived today.

Whether it is the lack of funding for education within black communities, to the banking system, where it is EXTREMELY difficult in acquiring business loans, we still see the ugly side of black prosperity until this day. And it is because of this continued mistreatment in regard to finances, why educating our youth, EARLY, with books like these are pivotal. Your generation has to get an earlier start in order to have a chance in your adult lives.

Let's Get It Started (LLC, Inc., Trademark, Copyrights, etc.)

If you take away anything from this book, I'd highly recommend it be the contents of this chapter. So, with that being said, let's get down to business. Speaking of business, the very first question you are going to have to answer is what type of business entity will your business be?

Before you choose what type of entity your business will be, you should know what it means. A business entity is the legal structure of your business. It determines your legal liability, if your business comes under fire. It determines the amount of taxes your company will have to pay.

There are several business entities to choose from. Those entities are:

Sole Proprietorship: This entity has one single owner, and that is YOU! You are personally, financially, and legally responsible, as the sole owner and operator of the business.

Partnership: With this entity, all the partners are responsible, if legal action is taken against the company. All parties are also responsible to report profits on personal taxes.

C Corporation: This business entity makes the business responsible if legal action is taken against. However, with this entity, you have government requirements to follow like creating bylaws, and holding board meetings. This entity is also taxed twice. The business is taxed, as well as personal earnings from company dividends.

S Corporation: This entity takes advantage of not being personally liable if legal actions are taken, while also not being taxed twice. One thing about this entity is it can only have one hundred shareholders, which prohibits the company from growing in size.

Limited Liability Company (LLC): This entity gives flexibility to how the business is taxed. It also separates the business from the owner. Government requirements, such as bylaws and board meetings, are not required with LLC's. Normally the best, and most selected choice, for small businesses, when selecting an entity.

Regardless of which entity you choose for your business, it is very important to make sure the right entity type for your business is selected, as your choice could set you up for success, as well as decrease the amount of risk for you, your business, and/or your partners, so choose wisely.

It May Cost You A Little, It May Cost You A lot, But IT WILL Cost You

Have you ever heard the phrase, "You have to spend money to make money?" This just means that there is a cost of doing business. Depending on what type of business you are in, will determine your biggest cost. Here are a few things you should consider when starting your business.

The entities that we discussed in the previous chapters are associated with a cost. Since most small businesses will start out utilizing the LLC route, let me give you some information on that.
In 2021, on the state of Maryland business site (see appendix), when I had just filed for an LLC, the initial filing paperwork cost me $196.73 ($191 filing fee + $5.73 nonrefundable service fee). There are also renewal fees, which you will pay on an annual basis which, depending on the state, cost between $50 - $75. These small fees are very necessary in making sure the name of your company is available for use, as well as protects you in case someone else attempts to use your name.

After the naming process, we must than discuss ways to make sure potential customers remember your business' name. This brings up marketing costs. One of those cost would be the biggest form of brand recognition, which is branding, more specifically, a logo.

The average graphic designer charges $100 to design a logo. If this is too expensive for you, there are options out there such as freelance graphic design work. This is a great option because you will always be able to find individuals who are passionate about designing and are always willing to provide designs at an affordable rate.

Making sure your logo is the best it can be is very important, and something that you must get right. Think of some of the greatest and most recognizable logos out there. Think about the golden arches, or the Nike check sign. People see these and AUTOMATICALLY know what they are. You want to make sure your logo does the same.

If you provide a service, then you are going to have to pay for the things you need to complete that service. If you cook/bake, you need ingredients. If you provide cleaning services, you are going to need cleaning supplies. If you are starting a clothing company, you are going to have to purchase the clothes in which you will be selling.

Years ago, when I started my clothing line, I found a manufacturer in New York City, who I spent thousands of dollars with, because I had to purchase in bulk. While I saved money on each shirt, hat, etc. by buying in bulk, I also learned a valuable lesson that translate across any venture. That lesson is that you MUST have customers who are going to purchase your product or use your service.

While I thought I had a great idea, and felt like I knew a bunch of people, I just automatically assumed that I would be able to sell one thousand shirts. I quickly realized that I was unable to, and unfortunately, was left with hundreds of shirts that I was not able to sell. This resulted in me having to sell the clothes at a much cheaper rate, or worse, not selling them at all, and just giving them away.

Products and goods, depending on what type of business you are starting, is the one cost that you may not be able to figure out in its entirety when starting out. There are so many factors, that you just won't be able to account for, particularly because you never been in business for yourself. However, just like you don't know all the factors that may make things cost, you also don't know about all the resources available to you.

Resources that include grant money, angel investors (someone providing startup money for future compensation, ownership, etc.), etc. Regardless, if it is an obstacle, or a resource, an asset, or a liability, all of it works together in determining how much money you will spend. It is the cost of doing business. It may cost you a little, or it may cost you a lot, but it is going to cost you.

Just Do It

If you have made it this far, then you have taken in a lot of information. Now, hopefully, you should know what an entrepreneur is. You should know what a business entity is, and the different types of business entities to choose from.

You learned so much today, but the one thing that cannot be taught, or learned, is what you do next. The information you received today was very simple, and easy to comprehend. It is some of the most valuable information you will ever receive. It is information I wish someone would have taught me when I was your age.

All the information you learned today, I had to learn on the fly. When I started my first business, it was very much trial and error. Today, you were given a head start. The question now is,

What are you going to do with it?

Arguably the most popular brand in the world is Nike. Their slogan is arguably the simplest, yet effective slogan ever, "JUST DO IT!" At the end of the day, there is so much more information that you can, and will learn, when starting a business. The one thing you will not have to learn is going with your gut. You think you have a great idea, act on it.

The world is waiting for the next big thing; however, no one has provided it yet. Why else do you think we have seen a surge in movies and television shows being remade? Why is it that Michael Jordan has not come out with any new shoes? All the Jordan brand has done is re-release shows made decades ago, just in different color schemes. This is because nothing new has been created.

Do not second guess yourself. If you think about it, start putting it into action. The only thing left to do is take Nike's advice, and JUST DO IT!

Things "TO DO"

☐ Make the decision to start a business

☐ Think of a passion of yours, and/or a need that you see.

☐ Name your business

☐ Pick your business structure (LLC., Corp., Etc.)

☐ Create business logo

☐ Pay for first production of products being sold, or first order of supplies, if providing a service.

☐ Set your price

☐ Let's Make Some Money

About the Author

Marcus W. Brewster learned how to effectively communicate by graduating from George Mason University with a Bachelor of Arts degree in Communications. He later learned his business acumen, by receiving his Masters in Business Administration from DeVry Keller Graduate School of Management.

With his education attained, it was only right that Marcus would be an entrepreneur. He is the owner of the clothing line, Victory Everywear, and Marcus of Ceremony, where he provides MC/Hosting Services. As an on-air personality, who goes by "Mr. Victory or Nothing," he is the founder of "Victory or Nothing, LLC" in which he hosts shows such as "The Moment of Victory," as well as release music under.

Despite all he does in Corporate America, and from an entrepreneurial standpoint, Marcus feels his greatest contribution to society is being a father. The same passion he has as a father, is the same passion he uses to uplift and inspire his community, particular the youth, through his acts of service.

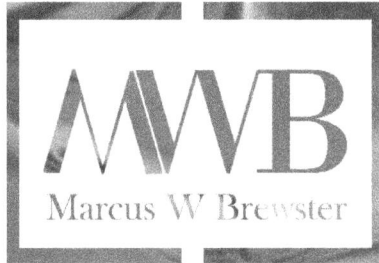

Instagram

@MarcusWBrewster

Twitter

@MarcusWBrewster

Facebook

Marcus Brewster

Web Inquiries

www.MarcusWBrewster.com